LOOK UP TODAY

By

Ora Mae Irving

ISBN: 0-75962-574-3

This book is printed on acid free paper.

1stBooks - rev. 04/09/01

"LOOK UP TODAY"

LOOK UP TODAY WHEN TROUBLES COMES...
BY YOUR PATH...
ALWAYS BE CHEERFUL...
AND BE GLAD...

FORGET THOSE PAINS AND SORROW...
KNEEL AND PRAY FOR TOMORROW...

LOOK UP WHEN THINGS
ARE NOT GOING YOUR WAY...
JESUS IS LOOKING DOWN ON YOU...
PRAYING FOR A BRIGHTER DAY...
DON'T GET DISCOURAGE WHEN GOD COMES FOR
ME...
I'VE DONE MY BEST, SO HE'S TAKING ME TO REST...

ANGELS ARE WAITING FOR ME TO TAKE ME BACK...
SO I CAN BE FREE...
I WITNESS DOWN HERE ON THIS EARTH...
I WITNESS TO MY LOVE ONES IN THIS EARTH...
MY FAMILY AND FRIENDS...
DON'T BE SAD JUST LOOK UP AND BE GLAD...

written by : Ora Irving

Ora Mae Irving

"ATTENTION FROM GOD"

**I WANT ATTENTION FROM GOD ALONE
EVEN THOUGH I KNOW I'M WRONG...**

**GOD GIVES ATTENTION TIME AFTER TIME
HE SAID "MY CHILD I'LL NEVER LEAVE YOU
BEHIND
I WILL ALWAYS BE AROUND"...**

**HE SAID "IF YOU WILL WAIT UNTIL YOUR TIME IS
HERE
YOU WILL HAVE ALL THE ATTENTION AND YOU
WON'T HAVE NO FEAR"
ATTENTION FORM GOD
IS BOUGHT WITH A PRICE...**

written by: Ora Irving

"TO MY PASTOR"

YOU'RE MY LEADER
EVERY STEP OF THE WAY
GOD GAVE YOU THE REVELATIONS
TO HELP ME EACH DAY...

WHEN I COME TO CHURCH
YOU TEACH THE WORD TO ME AND I LISTEN
BUT WHEN I STAY HOME
GOD'S HOLY WORD THAT'S WHAT I'M MISSING...

IT'S NOT YOUR FAULT
IF I GO TO HELL
YOU TAUGHT THE BIBLE
ALL SO WELL...

IF I WILL ONLY DO
WHAT THE BIBLE SAY
I KNOW I WILL MAKE IT TO HEAVEN
AND HAVE ETERNAL LIFE EVERYDAY...

written by: Ora Irving

"GOD IS ON THE ROAD"

WHEN YOU TRAVEL ON THE HIGHWAY
DO NO WORRY AND HAVE NO FEAR
MY GOD IS ALWAYS THERE AND NEAR...

GOD IS ON THE ROAD
ALL OF THE TIME
HE'S JUST WAITING ON A PHONE CALL
YOU HAVE LOST RECOGNITION...

GOD IS NOT ASLEEP
NEITHER GONE AWAY
HE'S JUST WAITING
TO HEAR YOU PRAY...

GOD IS IN THE CAR
ALL OF THE TIME
HE JUST WANT YOU
TO GIVE HIM SOME OF YOUR TIME...

IF YOU FALL ASLEEP
AT THE WHEEL
JUST REMEMBER
MY GOD STILL LIVES...

written by: Ora Irving

"GOD KNOWS YOU"

GOD KNOWS YOU AND
WHAT YOU'RE GOING THROUGH
HE KNOWS WHAT YOU WILL SAY AND DO...

HE KNOWS YOUR EVERYDAY LIFE
WHEN YOU TALK TO HIM
YOU CAN TELL GOD NO LIES...

GOD KNOWS YOUR MOVE DAY BY DAY
HE KNOWS WHEN YOU FALL ON
YOUR KNEES TO PRAY...

GOD KNOWS YOU WHEN YOU
PROMISE HIM YOU WILL CHANGE
BUT INSTEAD YOUR LIFE
REMAIN THE SAME...

GOD REALLY KNOWS
WHO YOU ARE ALL THE TIMES
HE KNOWS WHEN YOU ARE
TEARING HIM DOWN...

GOD KNOWS YOU!!!!

written by: Ora Irving

Ora Mae Irving

"HATE YOU DON'T NEED"

HATE YOU DON'T NEED
IN YOUR EVERYDAY LIFE
ASK THE LORD
TO TAKE IT AWAY WHEN IT ARRIVES...

HATE TRIES TO TAKE
OVER YOUR LIFE
FALL ON YOUR KNEES
AND HAVE THE LORD ON YOUR SIDE...

HATE YOU DON'T NEED
EVEN THOUGH YOU PRAY
HATE WILL MAKE YOU GO ASTRAY...

HATE WILL LEAVE YOU
ALL ALONG
WITH THE DEVIL LAUGHING
WHEN THINGS GO WRONG...

HATE YOU DON'T NEED
WHILE YOU'RE SITTING IN CHURCH
THE DEVIL'S POINTING HIS FINGERS
TRYING TO GET YOU, WHERE IT HURTS...

written by: Ora Irving

"WHEN I STOP TALKING"

WHEN I STOP TALKING
AT THE END OF MY LIFE
DON'T BE SAD AND CRYING
BECAUSE YOU KNOW I'M TIRED...

WHEN I STOP TALKING
AND CAN'T DO NOTHING
JUST REMEMBER ON THING TO SAY
WHEN SHE WAS UP, SHE DONE ALL SHE COULD...

WHEN I STOP TALKING
AND CAN'T SPEAK ANYMORE
JUST REMEMBER ONE THING TO SAY
SHE WITNESS TO MANY PEOPLE
AT THEIR OWN FRONT DOORS...

WHEN I STOP TALKING AND
CAN ONLY WAVE MY HAND
JUST REMEMBER ONE THING TO SAY
GOD IS IN HEAVEN
HE REMAINS THE SAME...

written by: Ora Irving

Ora Mae Irving

"GOD'S WORK"

WHEN I LOOK SO FAR WAY
I SEE THE SUN SHINING BRIGHT TODAY
THE CLOUDS ARE BLUE
THE BIRDS ARE FLYING IN THE AIR
I KNOW THERE IS A GOD UP THERE...

THAT'S GOD'S WORK!!!

WHEN I LOOK AROUND ME
TO SEE THE DOGS BARDING
THE COWS ARE MOOING
AND THE GOATS ARE CHEWING...

THAT'S GOD 'S WORK!!!

GOD'S WORK IS THE GREATEST
OF THEM ALL
NO ONE CAN TOUCH IT
NEVER, NOT AT ALL...

THE BABIES ARE BORN EVERYDAY
MOVING AND SMILING ALONG THE WAY
BABIES HAVE SPECIAL LOVE
COMING FROM GOD ABOVE...

THAT'S GOD'S WORK!!!

written by: Ora Irving

"A LIGHT SHINES ON ME"

A LIGHT SHINES ON ME AS I FALL ASLEEP
IT COMES FROM GOD ABOVE
HE'S LOOKING DOWN ON ME
WITH HIS PRECIOUS LOVE...

I DON'T NEED TO WORRY
ABOUT ANYONE HERE
THE ANGELS ARE MY GUIDE
SO I WON'T HAVE ANY FEAR...

I WAKE UP IN THE MORNING
GOING ON WITH MY DAILY WORK
A LIGHT SHINES ON ME
EVEN WHEN THINGS GET ROUGH...

A LIGHT SHINES ON ME EVERYDAY
EVEN WHEN I MAKE A MISTAKE
A LIGHT IS ALWAYS THERE, IT IS NEVER LATE...

written by: Ora Irving

Ora Mae Irving

"MY STEPS"

WHEN I WALK EVERY DAY
EACH STEP I TAKE
THE LORD HELP ME TO MAKE...

I TRY TO WALK STRAIGHT
ALONG THE WAY
SO I WON'T FALL
EACH AND EVERYDAY...

GOD TELLS ME WHERE
TO GO WHEN I WALK
SO THERE WILL BE
NO FAULT...

IF I WALK WITH GOD
AND KEEP MY STEPS STRAIGHT
MAYBE ONE DAY I WILL
MEET HIM AT THE ETERNAL GATE...

written by: Ora Irving

"WHEN I AM ON A TRIP"

WHEN I AM ON A TRIP
FAR AWAY FROM HOME
MY CAR HAS BROKEN DOWN
I NEED A LIFT...

RIDING THE HIGHWAY
DAY BY DAY
LOOKING AROUND
IT SEEMS LIKE ONLY YESTERDAY...

ALL MY FAMILY
RIDING WITH ME
I'M PLEASED
THE LORD IS WITH ME...

I SEE MANY THINGS
LIKE NEVER BEFORE
THERE IS NO PLACE LIKE HOME
WHEN I CAN LOOK OUT MY FRONT DOOR...

I MISS MY HOME VERY MUCH
THAT'S WHY I HAVE MANY OF FRIENDS
I CAN STAY IN TOUCH...

written by: Ora Irving

"NO ONE LIKE JESUS"

JESUS IS A MAN, AN UNMATCHABLE MAN
AND HE OWNS ALL OF THE LAND
HE WILL NEVER LET YOU FALL
NO MATTER WHAT, WHERE, OR WHEN
OR THE CAUSE...

THAT'S WHY NO ONE'S LIKE JESUS...
THAT'S WHY NO ONE'S LIKE THE LORD...

HE CAN CHANGE YOUR NIGHT IN TODAY
HE CAN MAKE THE DEVIL GET AWAY...

THAT'S WHY NO ONE'S LIKE THE LORD!!!

PROBLEMS IN YOUR LIFE, TIME AFTER TIME
MY JESUS IS ALWAYS GOING TO BE AROUND
TO GIVE YOU A CROWN
ALL YOU HAVE TO DO IS BOW AND PRAY
ONE THING ABOUT IT GODS ALREADY MADE THE
WAY...

THAT'S WHY NOBODY
NOBODY IS LIKE THE LORD!!!

written by: Ora Irving

"MY HEART"

MY HEART BELONGS TO JESUS
ALL OF THE TIME
EVEN WHEN TROUBLE TRIES
TO GET ME DOWN...

MY HEART PAINS ALONG THE WAY
DAY BY DAY,
IF I ONLY CALL GOD
HELP IS ON THE WAY...

MY HEART BELONGS TO JESUS
THIS I KNOW
WHEN I LOOK AROUND HE IS WITH ME
WHERE EVER I GO...

MY HEART HURTS SOMETIMES
THROUGH AND THROUGH
JESUS TOUCHED MY HEART
HE SAID "MY CHILD YOU KNOW I AM WITH YOU"...

GOD SAID IF YOU CARE
ABOUT YOUR HEART
THERE IS NO PROBLEM IN YOUR LIFE
THAT CAN'T BE SOLVED...

written by: Ora Irving

Ora Mae Irving

"SPECIAL SISTER"

SISTER YOU ARE SPECIAL TO ME
THE THINGS YOU DO
I CAN NEVER REPAY...

SISTER YU BEEN THERE FOR ME
MANY OF TIMES
THE TIMES WHEN I DIDN'T
HAVE A DIME...

YOU NEVER FORSAKEN ME
NO MATTER WHAT I'VE DONE
YOU JUST KEPT IT QUIET
AND TREATED ME LIKE I WAS SOMEONE SPECIAL...

SISTER, YOU ENCOURAGED ME
WHEN THINGS WERE GOING BAD
YOU STILL ENCOURAGED ME
WHEN I WAS GLAD...

I REALLY THANK THE LORD FOR YOU
YOU HAVE HELPED ME IN THE PAST TOO...

written by: Ora Irving

"MY LOVING DAUGHTER"

MY CHILD I LOVE YOU
ALL THE TIME MORE
THAN WORDS CAN SAY
WORDS, I COULDN'T FIND...

YOU'RE ONE SPECIAL CHILD
I THINK OF ALL THE TIME
EVEN THOUGH THERE WAS MANY TIMES
I HAD TO LEAVE YOU BEHIND...

I CARE FOR YOU
FROM THE BOTTOM OF MY HEART
SOMETHING I CAN'T EXPLAIN
IT SEEM SO VERY HARD, AND YOU BEING SO VERY
FAR...

YOU'RE SPECIAL OVER THE YEARS
WHEN I THINK OF ALL THE THINGS YOU BEEN
THROUGH
IT BRINGS ME MANY OF TEARS...

YOU'RE SPECIAL!!!!

written by: Ora Irving

"I'M YOUR GOD"

I GAVE MYSELF TO JESUS
A LONG TIME AGO
I BEEN SO PEACEFUL
WITH NO PAINS TO BEAR ANYMORE...

I DEDICATED MY WHOLE LIFE
TO JESUS, LIKE NEVER BEFORE
I WANT TO HAVE ETERNAL LIFE
AND THAT IS MY GOAL...

I'M YOUR GOD
ALL THE WAY
I WILL MEET YOU
AT JUDGEMENT DAY...

THERE IS NOTHING I WANT TO LOSE MY LIFE FOR
ONLY TO BE WITH YOU
BECAUSE OF YOUR EVERLASTING WORD
THAT IS TRUE...

written by: Ora Irving

"MY AUNT"

AUNT YOU WAS THERE
FOR ME EVERY SINCE I WAS A CHILD
YOU DIDN'T CRITICIZE
NOR PUSH ME ASIDE...

YOU ALWAYS GAVE ME THE VERY BEST
YOU BOUGHT ME CLOTHES LIKE I WAS YOUR
CHILD
THAT'S WHY I STAY IN YOUR LIFE...

I'LL NEVER FORGET
NO MATTER WHERE I GO
YOU WILL BE IN MY HEART EVERYDAY
I'LL NEVER FORGET YOU ANYMORE...

written by: Ora Irving

Ora Mae Irving

"I HAVE A TALENT"

I HAVE A TALENT
I CAN'T EXPLAIN
IT IS WORKING
THAT IS NO GAME...

THE TALENT I HAVE
IS AS BEAUTIFUL AS CAN BE
WHEN YOU READ IT
IT WILL LIFT YOU TO BE FREE...

IF YOU READ EVERY
WORD THAT I WRITE
IT WILL HELP YOUR BURDENS
TO BE LIGHT...

I'M NOT SELFISH
BECAUSE GOD GAVE ME THIS TALENT
TO TELL ALL THE WORLD
TO HELP OTHERS TO BE FREE...

written by: Ora Irving

"A NEW FRIEND"

A NEW FRIEND IS HARD TO FIND
IF YOU FIND ONE BE VERY KIND
KEEP A SMILE ON YOUR FACE
NO ONE CAN TAKE A NEW FRIEND'S PLACE...

WHEN YOU TALK
LOOK IN THEIR EYES
THEN YOU WILL SEE
WHAT THEY'RE THINKING INSIDE...

PUT YOUR ARMS AROUND THEM
AND SHOW THAT YOU CARE
YOUR LOVE IS NOT DIM
IT IS ALWAYS THERE...

A NEW FRIEND WILL LISTEN
WILL NOT WALK OUT
A NEW FRIEND NEVER SHOW
YOU ANY DOUBT...

A NEW FRIEND WILL SHARE THEIR THOUGHTS
WITHOUT FINDING ANY FAULT...

written by: Ora Irving

"A PLACE FOR ME"

THERE IS A PLACE WAITING FOR ME
WITH MY GOD NEAR TO THEE...

I'M GETTING READY EVERYDAY
I HOPE ONE DAY I GET MY PAY...

I WISH ALL MY LOVE ONES
CAN MEET ME THERE
WITH ANGELS STANDING EVERYWHERE...

WALKING AND TALKING
WITH LOVE ONE'S GONE ON BEFORE
I'M SURE THEY WILL BE
WAITING AT THE DOOR...

written by: Ora Irving

"A WOMAN OF GOD"

A WOMAN OF GOD
TO DO GOD WILL
SHE WILL GUIDE YOU ALONG
TO BE REAL...

SHE IS AS SWEET AS CAN BE
NEVER CHANGES, WHEN SHE WALK THE STREET...

SHE SPEAKS GOD WORD
THAT'S FOR SURE
IT WILL KEEP YOU THINKING
AND BRING MANY OF TEARS...

WHAT SHE SAY
WILL TOUCH YOUR HEART
UNTIL YOU WILL MAE A DECISION WITH GOD
AND NEVER DEPART...

SHE NEVER TURNS YOU AWAY
DAY OR NIGHT
NO PROBLEM TO BIG
SHE GOT GOD IN SIGHT...

THAT'S A WOMAN OF GOD!!!

written by: Ora Irving

"CHILDREN OF GOD"

CHILDREN OF GOD IS DOING GOD'S WORK
STAYING IN CHURCH TRYING TO GET A TOUCH...

CHILDREN OF GOD
PRAY EVERY CHANCE COME THEIR WAY
TRYING TO GET TO HEAVEN
ON JUDGMENT DAY...

SINGING AND SHOUTING
DAY BY DAY
TRYING TO GET CLOSER TO GOD
TO RECEIVE THEIR PAY...

THE CHILDREN OF GOD
WILL WITNESS EVERY TIME
AND THROUGH THE DAY ON THE TELEPHONE
AND ANY LINE...

CHILDREN OF GOD
ARE PECULIAR PEOPLE
THEY ARE DIFFERENT
AND DON'T MIND SWEEPING...

THEY ARE HONEST
AS CAN BE
THEY WILL PRAY TO GOD
TO SET THEM FREE...

written by: Ora Irving

"CHRISTMAS"

CHRISTMAS IS A SPECIAL DAY
I'LL THINK OVER MY LIFE
AND HOW GOD TAUGHT ME TO PRAY...

CHRISTMAS IS FULL OF JOY
BEING WITH FAMILY AND FRIENDS
TOGETHER THEY LOOK, LISTEN AND
PLAY WITH TOYS...

CHRISTMAS TIME WE SPEND
PLENTY OF MONEY
WHILE WE ARE SPENDING
WE ARE LAUGHING AND BUYING
THINGS THAT ARE SOMETIMES FUNNY...

WE WILL FORGET OUR BILLS
WE MUST PAY UNTIL AFTER
CHRISTMAS OR THE VERY NEXT DAY...

WE ARE WRAPPING GIFTS LIKE NEVER BEFORE
UNTIL SOMEONE COMES
AND KNOCK ON THE DOOR...

AFTER WE'VE ANSWER THE DOOR
WE KEEP WRAPPING GIFTS SOME MORE...

written by: Ora Irving

"A LITTLE COUNTRY GIRL"

I'M A LITTLE COUNTRY GIRL
FROM A SMALL TOWN
TRYING TO GET RICH
AND DON'T HAVE A DIME...

I KEEP ON TRYING
NEVER GIVING UP
WITH ALL MY DETERMINATION
IT'S STILL NOT ENOUGH...

I'M GOING ON LIKE NEVER BEFORE
HOPING ONE DAY SOMEONE WILL
KNOCK AT MY DOOR...

I'M A LITTLE COUNTRY GIRL
THAT'S WHAT I AM...

I DRESS DIFFERENT FROM ANYONE
SOME PEOPLE LOOK AT ME
BUT, I KEEP ON GOING
UNTIL I GET THE KEY
WHEN I GET THE KEY
I'LL BE ALRIGHT...

I'M A LITTLE COUNTRY GIRL
THAT'S WHAT I AM...

written by: Ora Irving

"FAMILIES TOGETHER"

FAMILIES COME TOGETHER
FROM TIME TO TIME
THEY SOMETIME FORGET
TO PRAY AND LEAVE GOD BEHIND...

GOD IS ALWAYS THERE
IN YOUR MIST
HE'S WAITING ON YOU
TO GIVE HIM YOUR LIST...

HE NEVER TURN YOU DOWN
NO MATTER WHAT YOUR PROBLEM IS
IF YOU WILL REMEMBER
MY GOD IS REAL...

GOD WANT THE BEST
FOR YOU IN YOUR LIFE
HE WANTS YOU TO PRAY MORE
AND GIVE HIM PLENTY OF YOUR TIME...

written by: Ora Irving

"FAMILY MEETING ME IN HEAVEN"

I WANT MY FAMILY
TO MEET ME IN HEAVEN
WHEN THEY GET THEIR SOUL'S RIGHT WITH GOD
WERE THINGS WILL BE BETTER...

I WILL BE THERE
THAT'S FOR SURE
MY SOUL'S BEEN WASHED WITH HIS BLOOD
NOW IT IS PURE...

I DON'T WANT TO LEAVE THEM
BUT, I MUST GO ON
I WILL SEE THEM IN HEAVEN
WHEN ALL THEIR WORK IS DONE...

SOONER OR LATER
WE WILL MEET AGAIN
WE CAN SING AND SHOUT
UP THERE IN HEAVEN...

written by: Ora Irving

"FATHER'S DAY"

FATHER YOU ARE MY FRIEND
YOU ARE ALWAYS THERE TO THE END
NO MATTER HOW I FALL
YOU HAVE NEVER COMPLAINED...

WHEN I SEE YOU
YOU HAVE NEVER CHANGED
I KNOW YOU WILL BE THE SAME
LISTENING AND LOOKING EVERYWHERE
I APPEAR...

NO MATTER HOW FAR I MAY BE
I CAN ALWAYS CALL ON YOU
YOU'RE A COMFORTER AND A GUIDE
NO MATTER WHAT MOVE I MAKE
YOU WILL BE ON MY SIDE...

YOU ARE TELLING ME
GOD'S WORK TO HELP ME ALONG THE WAY
NO MATTER WHERE I AM
YOU ARE SHOWING ME HOW TO PRAY...

I REMEMBER YOU SAYING
"THERE IS A BRIGHTER DAY"!!!

written by: Ora Irving

"FREEDOM"

I WANT TO TELL YOU A STREET STORY
ABOUT THIS GIRL SHE ON DRUGS AND HAD
MANY TROUBLES, ALWAYS WORRY...

SHE WAS SHAKING AND TREMBLING EVERYDAY
TRY TO GET A FIX ANYWAY...

SHE HAD A LINE OF GAMES YOU NEVER HEARD
BUT WHEN YOU TURNED YOUR BACK
SHE TURNED A CURVE...

SHE RUN SO FAST TO GET REAL HIGH
IF YOU SEE HER, SHE WANT TO FLY...

WHEN YOU TALK, SHE WOULD LAUGH AT YOU
AT EVERY WORD YOU SAY...

THIS IS WHAT I MEAN WHEN I SAY
THERE'S GOT TO BE A WAY OUT OF ANY DAY...

written by: Ora Irving

"GET BETTER SOON"

YOU CAN GET BETTER
WITH THE WORD OF GOD BY YOUR SIDE
AND IN YOUR LIFE...

YOU CAN GET BETTER
BY PUTTING GOD FIRST
HE IS THE ANSWER
AND GOD WILL SHOW HIS LOVE...

YOU CAN GET BETTER
BY LOOKING TO GOD
PUTTING YOUR TRUST IN HIM
GOD WILL NEVER DEPART...

GETTING BETTER
BY WALKING OUT ON FAITH
HE NEVER CHANGE
GOD IS ALWAYS THE SAME...

written by: Ora Irving

"GETTING CLOSER BY THE DAY"

WE ARE GETTING CLOSER
BY THE DAY
EVERYTHING YOU SAY
WILL MAKE ME HAPPY ALONG THE WAY...

YOU'RE GENTLE ALL THE TIME
I CAN'T LOSE YOU, BECAUSE YOU'RE MINE...

WE GET CLOSER AND CLOSER WHERE EVER WE GO
EVEN THE TIME WHEN YOU WALK OUT THE DOOR
SEPARATE US ANYMORE...

WE HAD SOME HARD TIMES
BUT I WANT YOU TO BE CLOSER
BY ME THE MAJORITY OF THE TIME...

WE SHARED ALL THE THINGS
THAT CAME OUR WAY
THE CLOSER WE GET
WE MUST CONTINUE TO PRAY...

written by: Ora Irving

"GOD IS IN MY HOME"

GOD IS IN MY HOME
EVERYDAY AS I KNEEL DOWN TO PRAY...

I THANK THE LORD
FOR FOOD I EAT
THEN I FALL SOUND TO SLEEP...

WHEN I RISE THE VERY NEXT DAY
I'M PRAYING THAT GOD
WILL HELP ME ON MY WAY...

GOD IS MY GUIDE AND MY FRIEND
HE'S ALWAYS WITH ME
UNTIL THE END...

GOD IS IN MY HOME ALL THE TIME
WAITING ON ME
TO LET MY LIGHT SHINE...

written by: Ora Irving

"GOD IS NEAR"

YOU DON'T NEED TO WORRY
YOU DON'T NEED TO FEAR
ONLY IF YOU PRAY
GOD IS ALWAYS NEAR...

HE'S LOOKING AT YOU
EVERYWHERE YOU GO
GOD IS ALWAYS THERE
KNOCKING AT YOUR DOOR...

REMEMBER WHEN HE DIED
ON THE CROSS FOR YOU
GOD WAS HOPING ONE DAY
YOU WILL HAVE AN ETERNAL HOME TOO...

HE NEVER CHANGES
WHAT HE SAID
JUST REMEMBER MY FRIENDS
GOD IS ALWAYS THERE...

written by: Ora Irving

"GOD SHOW ME THE WAY"

WHEN I LOOK IN THE SKY
ASKING THE LORD THE REASON WHY
PAINS AND SUFFERING EVERYDAY
HOPING THE LORD WILL SHOW ME THE WAY...

I HEAR MUSIC IN MY EARS
SWEET MEMORIES OF MY LOVE
ONE WITHOUT MANY TEARS
HE IS HERE AND EVERYWHERE
I DON'T HAVE TO WORRY ANYMORE OR FOREVER...

GOD SHOWED ME THE WAY MAN OF TIMES
I CHOSE THE WORLD OVER GOD
BECAUSE I DIDN'T WANT TO LEAVE MY LOVE ONES
BEHIND...

GOD SHOWED ME THE ROAD
TO THE HEAVENLY GATES
INSTEAD OF DOING HIS WILL
I ALWAYS TRIED TO GET A DATE...

THE ROAD SEEM LONG
AND THE WAY IS HARD
GOD SHOWED ME THIS WORD
SO I WON'T DEPART...

written by: Ora Irving

"GOD'S GIFT"

GOD GAVE ME THIS GIFT
THAT'S ALL I KNOW
WHEN I GREW UP
I WAS VERY POOR...

GOD LOOKED ON ME AND SAID
THAT'S MY CHILD
I'LL WORK THROUGH HER
WHILE SHE WRITES AND TOUCH OTHER'S LIVES...

I DIDN'T CHANGE BECAUSE I COULD WRITE
POETRY
I JUST KEPT ON PRAYING AND PUTTING MY POEMS
IN GOD'S HAND...

IF THIS IS WHAT
GOD WANT ME TO DO
HE TOUCHED THE RIGHT PERSON'S HEART
TO SEE ME THROUGH...

written by: Ora Irving

"HEAVENLY ROAD"

HEAVENLY ROAD
IS LONG AS CAN BE
TO SEE JESUS
STANDING WITH THEE...

TO TRAVEL THIS ROAD
YOU GOT TO BE RIGHT
SO YOU CAN SEE THE
ETERNAL LIGHT...

HEAVENLY ROAD IS A PEACEFUL ROAD
JUST SHAKE OFF THE DEVIL
AND HIS LOAD...

THERE WILL BE SINGING AND PRAYING
PLENTY OF INSTRUMENTS
AND GOD'S HOLY BAND...

YOU WILL BE GLAD
WHEN YOU GET THERE
NO MORE TROUBLE
NO MORE PAIN ANYWHERE...

written by: Ora Irving

"OUR HOUSE ON A HILL"

OUR HOUSE IS ON A HILL VERY SMALL
CHICKENS AND DUCKS EVERYWHERE
LAYING EGGS, HERE AND THERE...

FLOWERS ARE BLOOMING EVERYDAY
I KEEP ON PLANTING THEM ALONG THE WAY...

IN THIS HOUSE
MY FAMILY HAVE LOVE
ALL COMING FROM GOD ABOVE...

WE SHARE OUR THOUGHTS EVERYDAY
TRYING TO KEEP CLOSER DAY BY DAY...

written by: Ora Irving

"I CARE FOR YOU"

I CARE FOR YOU
BECAUSE YOU ARE SO
SWEET AND GENTLE
I DON'T KNOW WHAT I'LL DO...

WHEN I SEE YOU
I HAVE TO SMILE
I WAS IN LOVE WITH YOU
SINCE I WAS A CHILD...

YOU MAKE ME MOVE
VERY FAST, WITH KISSES
AND HUGS THAT WILL LAST...

YOU CAN ROCK MY WORLD
AT ANYTIME
I KNOW, I WON'T BE LEFT BEHIND...

I CARE FOR YOU, DAY AND NIGHT
WHEREVER YOU GO, I WON'T
LET YOU GET OUT OF MY SIGHT.

written by: Ora Irving

"I LOOK BEYOND"

WHEN I LOOK BEYOND
I SEE MANY OF THINGS
SOME THINGS ON THIS EARTH
I CAN'T EXPLAIN...

I LOOK SO FAR
JUST LIKE IT'S NEAR
HOPING ONE DAY
EVERYTHING WILL BECOME REAL...

I SEARCH AND SEARCH
FOR WHAT I'VE SEEN
BUT WHEN IT COMES
IT'S JUST LIKE A DREAM...

I LOOKED BEYOND
EVERYTHING AND MY SECRETS WASN'T HID...

written by: Ora Irving

"I LOST MY BEST FRIEND"

I LOST A FRIEND
SWEET AS CAN BE
NO ONE CAN TAKE THEIR PLACE
FOREVER WITH ME...

I LOST THE BEST FRIEND
THAT I EVER HAD
EVERY DAY GOES BY
IT MAKES ME VERY SAD...

I THOUGHT THAT I
WOULD NOT WORRY
ABOUT HER ETERNAL HOME
BUT EVERY DAY PAST
I'M LEFT HERE ALL ALONE...

I HOPE SHE HAVE MADE IT
TO HEAVEN GATES
THEN I WON'T WORRY
I'LL KNOW IT'S NOT TO LATE...

written by: Ora Irving

"I LOVE YOU"

I LOVE YOU BECAUSE YOU ARE YOU
WITHOUT YOU I DON'T' KNOW WHAT I WILL DO...

YOU'RE SPECIAL AS CAN BE
WHEN I SEE YOU MY HEART SKIPS A BEAT...

YOU WALK A WALK
LIKE NO OTHER MAN
YOU MOVE ME AND TAKE ME ON A FLIGHT...

YOU LOVE ME AND GIVE ME WHAT I NEED
I KNOW FOR SURE MY HEART IS PLEASED...

I GET WARM CHILLS
WHEN THINKING ABOUT YOU
A SPECIAL FEELING AND LOVING TOO...

written by: Ora Irving

"IF YOU KNOW"

WHEN YOU LOOK AT ME THROUGH THE DAY
SO MUCH PAIN
ALONG THE WAY...

IF YOU KNOW HOW I MADE IT
WHEN YOU LOOK BACK OVER MY LIFE
YOU'LL SAY SHE JUST DON'T SHOW IT...

IF YOU KNOW THE SORROW
WHEN YOU LOOK AROUND
THERE'S HOPE FOR TOMORROW...

IF YOU KNOW THE SUFFERING
I HAVE HAD WHEN GOD COME
FOR ME, YOU WILL SAY I'M
SO GLAD SHE IS FREE...

written by: Ora Irving

"I'M A WINNER"

I'M A WINNER THIS I KNOW
I NEVER GIVE UP ALWAYS KNOCKING
ON SOMEONE DOOR...

I NEVER STOP
NO MATTER WHAT OTHERS SAY
IF I KEEP GOING ON
HELP IS ON THE WAY...

I'M A WINNER
ALL THE TIME
WHEN I RISE IN THE MORNING
I'M ALWAYS ON TIME...

EVERYTHING IS IN PLACE FOR ME
IF I MAKE AN EFFORT
I WILL SUCCEED...

I'M A WINNER AT MY GAME
NO MATTER WHAT OTHER'S SAY
OR DO, I'M NEVER ASHAMED...

I'M A WINNER IN THE MORNING
NOON, EVENING AND NIGHT
ALWAYS PRAYING THAT EVERYTHING
WILL BE ALRIGHT...

I MADE IT THROUGH!!!

written by: Ora Irving

"I'M A WRITER"

I'M A WRITER
THAT'S WHAT I AM
THINKING EVERYDAY ABOUT ANYTHING...

I WRITE EVERYDAY
ALONG THE WAY
I WRITE ABOUT PEOPLE
AND WHAT THEY SAY...

I CARE ABOUT HOW IT SOUNDS
AS I WRITE
LISTENING AND LOOKING
FOR THE RIGHT WORDS TO BE FOUND...

I KEEP ON WRITING DAY BY DAY
UNTIL I HEAR MY PUBLISHER SAY
"I LIKE WHAT IT SAYS"...

I'M GOING TO BE THE BEST
AT WHAT I DO
WRITING POEMS ALL ABOUT YOU...

written by: Ora Irving

Ora Mae Irving

"I'M LEAVING YOU"

I'M LEAVING YOU MY CHILD
NO MORE PAINS TO BEAR ON THIS SIDE
I'VE HAD ENOUGH IN THIS LIFE...

I'VE HAD MY SHARE
OF LIFE'S UPS AND DOWNS
I'LL SEE YOU AGAIN
WHEN I GET MY CROWN...

I'M SORRY MY CHILD
I WILL REST WITH MY
GOD FOR A WHILE...

I'M JUST SLEEPING
AND GETTING MY REST
IT IS ONLY JUST A TEST...

NOW YOU CAN PRAY
TO GOD FOR YOURSELF
UNTIL YOU GET THROUGH
DON'T TURN TO NOBODY ELSE...

written by: Ora Irving

"I'M NOT TIRED"

I'M NOT TIRED AS I RISE
I KNOW THAT YOU LORD
ARE BY MY SIDE...

YOU LOOK ON ME
FROM DAY TO DAY
EVEN THOUGH SOMETIMES
I FORGET TO PRAY...

I'M NOT TIRED
OF CALLING YOUR NAME
TO HELP ME, EVEN THOUGH
SOMETIME'S I'M ASHAMED...

I'M NOT TIRED
OF BEING A WITNESS ON THE STREETS
TO DO GOD'S WILL
AS LONG AS I SHALL LIVE...

written by: Ora Irving

"I'M SAVE"

I'M SAVE THIS I KNOW
THE CHANGE I MADE
GOD IS TILL HELPING ME TO GROW...

I LOVE THE LORD
HE SAVED MY SOUL
I WANT TO LIVE RIGHT
AND BE MADE WHOLE...

I'M SAVE EVERYDAY
THAT'S WHY I DON'T MIND
KNEELING TO PRAY...

HE SAVED ME A MIGHTY LONG TIME AGO
JESUS IS MY HELPER I REALLY KNOW...

I GOT JOY ALL THE TIME
THINKING ABOUT JESUS
HOW HE MADE MY LIFE SHINE...

written by: Ora Irving

"I'M SORRY MOTHER"

I'M SORRY MOTHER
FOR THE THING I DID TO YOU
YOU KEPT ME IN PRAYER
AND LIFTED MY BURDENS TOO...

I'M SORRY MOTHER
HOW I MADE YOU CRY
I WAS SO IN SIN
I COULDN'T SEE WHY...

I'M SORRY MOTHER
YOU BENDED OVER YOUR BACK
TO HELP ME
BUT, I WILL TELL THE WORLD
YOU HAVE NEVER LEFT ME...

I'M SORRY MOTHER
I KNOW I'LL NEVER
GET ANOTHER MOTHER LIKE YOU
YOUR LOVE FOR ME IS ALWAYS TRUE...

I'M SORRY!!!!

written by: Ora Irving

"IT'S ME LORD"

IT WAS ME LORD
CRYING EVERY DAY
IT WAS ME LORD
WHO GOT DOWN ON MY KNEES TO PRAY...

IT WAS ME LORD
WHO WITNESS TO SOULS
IT WAS ME LORD
WHO WENT OUT IN THE COLD...

IT WAS ME LORD
WHO SPREAD THE WORD ABOUT YOU
IT WAS ME LORD
WHO SAID, "I'M GOING THROUGH"...

IT WAS ME LORD
WITH HELD UP HANDS
EVEN THOUGH THINGS WAS ROUGH...
IT WAS ME LORD
WITH SMILES EVERYDAY
I KEPT ON PRAYING
KNOWING HELP WAS ON THE WAY...

written by: Ora Irving

"IT'S NOT TIME"

I TRY TO PLAN THINGS EVERYDAY
SEEM LIKE NOTHINGS COMING MY WAY...

SEARCHING FOR AN ANSWER
ALONG THE WAY
SOMETIMES, I NEVER REALIZE
IT'S JUST NOT TIME...

I KEEP ON SEARCHING
TRYING TO FIND AN ANSWER
WHILE I WORK THINGS
JUST DON'T HAPPEN
IT'S JUST NOT TIME...

IT'S NOT TIME TO
PUT YOUR PLAN ON
WHEN FAILING AND EVERYTHING'S GOING WRONG
IT'S NOT TIME...

written by: Ora Irving

Ora Mae Irving

"IT'S NOT TO LATE"

IT'S NOT TO LATE
TO MAKE A START
WHEN YOU TRY
TO DO YOUR BEST
GOD WILL HELP YOU TO DO THE REST...

IT'S NOT TO LATE
TO SPEAK UP
WHEN THINGS ARE GETTING VERY TOUGH...

YOU HAVE A CHANCE
IN THIS LIFE
JUST KEEP ON GOING
AND DON'T HAVE PRIDE...

IT'S NOT TO LATE
TO SAY I MADE IT
AT LAST, JUST REMEMBER
THOSE DOUBT'S I HAD
WAS IN THE PAST...

written by: Ora Irving

"LOOKING ON"

WHEN YOU'RE SITTING AT HOME
AND BURDENS GET YOU DOWN
YOU DON'T NEED TO WORRY
GOD IS ALWAYS AROUND...

THINK OF HIS GOODNESS
AND ALL HE HAS DONE
HE BROUGHT YOU THROUGH
JUST KEEP ON LOOKING
AND SEE GOD IS WITH YOU...

LATE AT NIGHT WHEN I AWAKE
I ASK THE LORD FOR HELP
HE LOOKS ON ME WITHOUT A DOUBT...

LOOK ON DOWN THE ROAD
FOR YOUR BLESSING
NO MATTER HOW HARD IT SEEMS
JESUS IS THERE IN YOUR DREAMS...

JUST LOOK ON!!!!

written by: Ora Irving

"VALENTINE GIFT"

YOU ARE MY VALENTINE
SWEET AS CAN BE
I HOPE IN YOUR HEART
THERE IS ONLY LOVE FOR ME...

IN MY HEART
LOVE IS ONLY FOR YOU
IF I LOOSE YOU
WHAT WOULD I DO...

YOU ARE LIKE SWEET CANDY
ALL THE TIME
YOU ARE LIKE A PLENTY OF ROSES
THAT GROWS ON A VINE...

WHEN YOU COME AND GO
THE LOVE I HAVE FOR YOU
WILL NEVER GO...

I SEE FLOWERS THAT BLOOM EVERYDAY
THE LOVE I HAVE FOR YOU
WILL NEVER GO AWAY...

written by: Ora Irving

"WHEN I FOUND GOD"

WHEN I FOUND GOD
AND PUT HIM IN MY LIFE
EVERYTHING CHANGED
AND GOD WAS MY GUIDE...

I NEVER FORGET TO PRAY
EVERYDAY HE WAS AT MY SIDE
AND TAUGHT ME ALONG THE WAY...

GOD NEVER CHANGE
OR TURN ME AWAY
HE KEEP ON GUIDING ME
AND HEARD EVERY WORD I SAY...

THINGS WAS BETTER IN MY LIFE
WHEN I DEPENDED ON JESUS
AND NEVER GET TIRED...

I RISE EARLY IN THE MORNING
AND TALK WITH HIM
ON MY KNEES
I FELT HIS SPIRIT WILL NEVER LEAVE...

written by: Ora Irving

"WHEN I RISE"

WHEN I RISE THROUGH THE DAY
SEEING WHAT I CAN ACCOMPLISH
ALONG THE WAY...

I LOOK TO FIND SOMEONE I CAN
HELP EVEN THOUGH THEY MAY NOT
HAVE A DIME...

I FEEL RIGHT WITHIN MYSELF
KNOWING I HAVE A GOOD DEED
THAT HASN'T LEFT...

I WONDER WHY I RISE ABOVE
GOD GAVE A GIFT TO HELP EVERYONE
AND TO SHOW MY LOVE...

written by: Ora Irving

"WHEN I WAS A CHILD"

WHEN I WAS A CHILD
I FELT ALL ALONE
MY PARENTS WOULD TOUCH MY HEART
WHEN I WAS HOME...

THEY TAUGHT ME THE BIBLE
AND HOW TO LOVE EVERYBODY
IT WAS HARD FOR ME TO SEE
WHEN I GREW UP
IT HELPED ME TO BE FREE...

I WENT TO CHURCH
WHEN I WAS A CHILD
I SAT ON A BENCH AND HEARD MY FATHER
PREACH...

I DIDN'T MOVE, OR GO TO SLEEP
HE WANTED ME TO LISTEN
AND LEARN WHAT HE WOULD TEACH...

I THOUGHT IT WAS BAD
AT THE TIME
AS I GOT OLDER
I AM VERY GLAD...

written by: Ora Irving

"YOU'RE NEVER ALONE"

LOOKING AROUND FROM DAY TO DAY
TROUBLE IN THE LAND EVERYWHERE
I REMEMBER GOD'S WORK AS I GO THROUGH THE
DAY
I JUST REALIZE HE WANT ME TO PRAY...

YOU'RE NOT ALONE CAN YOU SEE
WHEN YOU GO THROUGII SUFFERING, PAIN, AND
SORROW
ETERNAL LIFE WITH JESUS
HE HAS SET YOU FREE...

YOU'RE NOT ALONE, IT'S JUST A TEST
HE WANT YOU TO LIVE RIGHT AND GIVE YOUR
BEST
WHEN LEAVING THIS WORLD AND FRIENDS BEHIND
YOU'VE WON THE VICTORY OVER SATAN
AND WON YOUR CROWN...

IT'S UP TO YOU TO BE CLOSE WITH HIM
HE IS ALWAYS BY YOUR SIDE
BECAUSE HE NEVER DIE
YOU'RE NOT ALONE FROM DAY TO DAY
JUST LOOK UP AND ALWAYS PRAY
YOU'RE NOT ALONE
JUST KEEP LOOKING UP AND BE VERY STRONG...

written by: Ora Irving

"YOU'RE SPECIAL"

YOU'RE SPECIAL TO ME
NO MATTER WHERE YOU ARE
I MISS YOU ALL THE TIME
MOST OF ALL WHEN YOU LEAVE TOWN...

YOU'RE SPECIAL BECAUSE
YOU ARE MY FRIEND
THE LOVE I HAVE FOR YOU
IT WILL NEVER END...

YOU'RE SPECIAL BECAUSE
YOU NEVER CHANGE
NO MATTER WHERE I AM EVEN IF I'M IN PAIN
YOU'RE ALWAYS THE SAME...

YOU'RE SPECIAL TO ME
NO MATTER WHERE I AM
YOU'RE SPECIAL...

written by: Ora Irving

"THE FLOWERS FROM GOD"

THE FLOWERS FROM GOD IS SPECIAL
THE GROW ON THEIR OWN
WITH NO WATER FROM OUR HOMES...

THEY BLOSSOM EVERYDAY
YOU CAN PICK THEM UP
AND WILL NOT HAVE TO PAY...

WHEN YOU SMELL THEM
THEY'RE SO SWEET
JUST LIKE SOME FOOD WE
SIT AND EAT...

THEY'RE FULL ALL THE TIMES
SOMETHING THAT YOU TREASURE
AND LOVE TO BE AROUND...

written by : Ora Irving

"I'M REACHING OUT"

I'M REACHING OUT
TOWARD THE WORLD
WITH A SPEECH OF POEMS
AND SOME FINE PEARLS...

I'M BOUNCING AND MOVING
EVERYDAY
THE WORDS THAT COMES TO ME
AND WHAT TO SAY...

TRYING TO TOUCH OTHER'S LIVES
WITH SOFT WORDS IN MY BOOK
WILL ALSO BE YOUR GUIDE...

THE THINGS I EXPERIENCE
WAS ONLY A TEST
THE LORD JUST WANTED ME
TO GIVE MY BEST...

written by : Ora Irving

"JESUS IS GREAT"

JESUS IS GREAT IN EVERYTHING HE DO
ONLY IF YOU PRAY
HE WILL SEE YOU THROUGH...

HE NEVER SLEEP OR SAY NO
WHEN YOU CALL HIM
GOD ISN'T SLOW...

REPENT OF YOUR SIN
THAT'S DONE EVERYDAY
SO WHEN YOU PRAY
GOD WILL HEAR WHAT YOU SAY...

JESUS KEEPS HARM
FROM COMING YOUR WAY
THE ANGELS ARE WATCHING EVERY DAY...

written by : Ora Irving

"MY CUP IS FILLED WITH LOVE"

MY CUP IS FILLED
WITH PLENTY OF LOVE
ALL COMING FROM GOD ABOVE...

THE LOVE IS RUNNING
FROM MY HEART EVERY DAY
CONTINUE TO COME
WHEN EVER I PRAY...

I CAN'T SHOW IT
WITHOUT MY GOD
HE'S ALWAYS THERE
AND NEVER DEPARTS...

THE CUP IS FULL OF LOVE
PURE AND SWEET THAT GIFT OF GOD
ARE FROM ABOVE...

written by : Ora Irving

Ora Mae Irving

"MOTHER'S DAY"

MOTHER YOU'RE MY FRIEND
YOU BEEN WITH ME THROUGH
THICK AND THIN
WHEN I HAD UPS AND DOWN
YOU WAS VERY CLOSE AROUND...

YOU NEVER TURNED ME DOWN
EVEN IF I WASN'T AROUND
YOUR HEART WAS THERE
THROUGHOUT THE DAY...

MOTHER YOU LOVED ME
WHEN I WAS WRONG
YOU KEPT ME UP IN PRAYER
HOPING GOD WILL HELP ME TO BE STRONG...

YOU WAS A COUNSEL
IN THE TIME OF NEED
ASKING GOD TO HELP ME
MOTHER, YOU ASKED ME
WHAT IS WRONG
AND YOU LISTEN TO MY PROBLEMS

YOU STILL ENCOURAGE ME
TO BE STRONG...

written by: Ora Irving

"MY DOG"

MY DOG IS PRETTY
AS CAN BE
RUNNING AND PLAYING
AROUND THE TREE...

BARKING AT STRANGE PEOPLE
WALKING ABOUT TRYING TO GET MY ATTENTION
WHEN I ARISE...

MY DOG LOVE TO EAT
AND WANT ATTENTION
WHEN WAKING UP AND COMING TO ME
I RUB MY DOG HEAD
AND HE GOES BACK TO SLEEP...

written by: Ora Irving

Ora Mae Irving

"MY DREAMS"

I HAVE DREAMS OF MANY THINGS
SOMETIMES I CAN'T EXPLAIN...

TOSSING AND TURNING
FROM SIDE TO SIDE
SEEING THINGS OF OTHER'S LIVES...

TRYING TO GET COMFORTABLE ANYWAY
WHEN I ARISE
WISHING FOR A BETTER DAY...

DREAMS COME TO ME IN MY SLEEP
AND WHEN I ARISE
THERE ARE THINGS I CAN REACH...

written by: Ora Irving

"MY GOAL"

MY GOAL IS TO GO TO THE TOP
TO KEEP LOOKING FORWARD
AND NEVER STOP...

LOOKING FOR MY DREAM
PRESSING ON UP THE ROAD
WHEN I GET AN ANSWER
I CAN RELEASE MY LOAD...

MY GOAL IS TO KEEP ON PUSHING
HIGHER AND HIGHER
UNTIL REACH MY GOAL
TO THE HIGHEST POWER...

I'M DETERMINED TO MAKE IT
I WILL NOT LET ANYTHING GET IN MY WAY
NOT RIGHT NOW
OR ANY OTHER DAY...

I CAN HEAR
NEEDING WORDS FROM MY LORD
IF I KEEP ON
I WILL GET MY PAY...

written by: Ora Irving

Ora Mae Irving

"MY KITCHEN"

MY KITCHEN IS SMALL
AS CAN BE
I'M SITTING AT THE TABLE
EATING WITH PEACE...

I LOVE MY KITCHEN
AND THE CURTAINS
HAVING MANY OF FLOWERS
AND COLORS OF BLUE...

PICTURES AND PAINTINGS
ON EVERY WALL
THEY ARE ALL IN PLACE
AND WILL NOT FALL...

I LOOK AROUND AT MY FLOOR
TRIMMED IN WHITE AND
PLENTY OF GOLD...

written by: Ora Irving

"PEACEFUL HOME"

A PEACEFUL HOME IS HARD TO FIND
WITH LOVING AND CARING YOU CAN'T FIND...

A PEACEFUL HOME IS AS SWEET AS CAN BE
WITH FRIENDS AND FAMILY
SITTING AND DRINKING COFFEE...

A PEACEFUL HOME IS TALKING AND DISCUSSING
TRYING TO MAKE THINGS HAPPY
WITHOUT A PLENTY OF FUSSING...

A PEACEFUL HOME IS PAYING BILLS ON TIME
SO YOU WON'T GET IN DEBT OR A YEAR BEHIND...

A PEACEFUL HOME IS ALL WE NEED
DON'T FORGET GOD AND PRAYER
GO DOWN ON YOUR KNEES...

written by: Ora Irving

"SEARCHING FOR AN ANSWER"

WHEN YOU'RE SEARCHING FOR AN ANSWER
ALL THE TIME
WHEN YOU'RE RISING IN THE MORNING
DON'T LEAVE GOD BEHIND...

IF YOU PRAY BEFORE YOU GO OUT
EVERYTHING WILL COME TOGETHER
LIKE A BRAND NEW DAY WITHOUT A DOUBT...

THE ANSWER YOU NEED IS WAITING ON YOU
JUST MAKE A CHANGE THEN YOU WILL SEE...

YOU'RE SEARCHING AND SEARCHING
FORGETTING TO ASK GOD FOR WHAT YOU WANT
FROM ABOVE
HE WILL ANSWER ALL YOUR QUESTIONS WITH HIS
HOLY WORD...

WHEN YOU GET THE ANSWER TO ALL YOUR NEEDS
DON'T FORGET ABOUT GOD
REMEMBER TO FALL ON YOUR KNEES...

written by: Ora Irving

"SHADOW"

I SEE A SHADOW
THE IMAGE OF MAN
MAKING ME AFRAID
AND I'M BREATHING FAST AS I CAN...

IF I WILL STAND STILL
THE LORD WILL LET ME SEE IT'S NOT REAL
IT'S JUST SOMETHING THERE
TO TEST MY FAITH...

IF I WAIT HE'LL DO THE REST
SHADOWS, I SEE EVERYWHERE
I DON'T WORRY GOD KNOWS BEST...

written by: Ora Irving

"SPECIAL OCCASION"

I LOOK FORWARD TO THIS DAY
TO MAKE MY LIFE WORTHWHILE
I KEEP ON PLANNING AND NEVER GET TIRED...

THIS DAY IS SPECIAL TO ME
IN EVERY WAY
I'M ASKING THE LORD
TO HELP ME EVERYDAY...

ALL MY FRIENDS AND FAMILY
ARE AT MY SIDE
DOING ALL THAT THEY CAN AND
NEVER HAVE PRIDE...

THIS OCCASION IS SPECIAL
SO I CAN MAKE MY SPEECH
HOPING TO GET RECOGNITION FORM OTHERS
AND SOULS I MIGHT REACH...

written by: Ora Irving

"SUCCESSFUL ON YOUR JOB"

I HOPE YOU ARE SUCCESSFUL
AS CAN BE
SHOW LOVE WITH NEW WORKERS
THAT DWELL INSIDE...

DON'T BE MEAN
NO MATTER WHAT HAPPENS
JUST SHOW LOVE AND WORK AS A TEAM...

REMEMBER TO PRAY
ALONG THE WAY
SO GOD CAN TOUCH YOUR BOSS MIND
TO LET YOU STAY...

DON'T FEEL BAD
WHEN YOU CAN'T HAVE YOUR WAY
JUST REMEMBER TO FALL ON YOUR KNEES AND
PRAY...

written by: Ora Irving

Ora Mae Irving

"THANKFUL FOR A NEW BABY"

A NEW BORN BABY IS AS PRECIOUS AS CAN BE
COMING FROM GOD WITH LOVE UNTO THEE...

A BABY IS HUMBLE AND FULL OF TUMBLE
LIKES TO ROLL ON THEIR TUMMY
A NEWBORN BABY
SMILE AND CRY
MOM ALWAYS WONDER WHY...

THANKFUL TO GOD
FOR THE NEW BORN IS NORMAL
A NEWBORN IS FRIENDLY AS CAN BE
IF WE WILL FOLLOW THEM
THE LESSON WILL SET US FREE...

THANKFUL TO GOD
FOR THE NEW BORN BABY WITH GOD TOUCH
THEY COME ON EARTH AND IS LOVED VERY
MUCH...

written by: Ora Irving

"TO MY SON"

MY SON YOU HAVE BEEN THERE FOR ME
EVEN WHEN YOU ARE FAR AWAY
I SILL THINK OF YOU EVERYDAY...

YOU HAVE HELPED ME EACH YEAR
I THANK THE LORD FOR A SON LIKE YOU
SO DEAR...

YOU HAVE BOUGHT ME MANY GIFTS
AND COMING FROM A SON LIKE YOU
IT GIVES ME A BIG LIFT...

YOU'RE MY SON THAT I LOVE SO MUCH
I HOPE YOU WILL NEVER CHANGE
AND STAY IN TOUCH...

MOST OF MY BLESSINGS
COME FROM YOU
REMEMBER TO PRAY AND
THE LORD WILL SEE YOU THROUGH...

written by: Ora Irving

"THE DAY I TURNED FROM GOD"

THE DAY I TURNED FROM GOD
I HAD IT VERY HARD
NOTHING WENT RIGHT
I JUST COULDN'T SEE THE LIGHT...

I HAD MANY OF FRIENDS ALL OF THE TIME
THE MOMENT I LEFT GOD
I WAS SEPARATED AND APART...

I TRIED TO CHANGE MY LIFE
LEAVING GOD OUT
I FORGOT TO PRAY
THE VERY SAME DAY...

THE DAY I TURNED FROM GOD
NOTHING SEEM THE SAME
I REALIZED I FORGOTTEN GOD
WAS THE MAN...

written by: Ora Irving

"IT'S FOR ME"

IT'S FOR ME TO GO ALL THE WAY
TO THE TOP AND NEVER STOP
TO WIN AND TO DO MY BEST...

IT'S FOR ME NOT TO CHANGE
WITH EVERY EFFORT IT WILL REMAIN THE SAME...

I GAVE MY BEST LIVING RIGHT
LEAVING IT TO GOD
HE HAVE TOOK ME TO THE LIGHT...

IT'S FOR ME
IF I PUT GOD FIRST IN MY LIFE
ALL OF THE TIME
EVEN WHEN I HAVE TO STRIVE...

IT'S FOR ME TO TURN AROUND
FROM MY OLD FASHIONED WAYS
TO LET GOD HELP ME
EACH AND EVERYDAY...

written by: Ora Irving

"COMING TOGETHER"

WE ARE COMING TOGETHER AS FRIENDS
LOVING EACH OTHER
WITH EVERYTHING THAT'S OUT AND WITHIN...

SEEKING GOD'S HELP FROM DAY TO DAY
AS WE FALL ON OUR KNEES AND PRAY...

TOGETHER WE ARE
NO MATTER HOW FAR
EVEN WHEN WE ARE DRINKING IN OUR CAR...

WE ARE TOGETHER LIKE NEVER BEFORE
EVEN WHEN SATAN KNOCKS ON OUR DOOR...

TOGETHER WE ARE ONE DAY SOON
TO GO WHERE THE LORD AND THERE WILL BE
ROOM...

written by: Ora Irving

"GOD WITH ME'

GOD IS HERE ALL THE TIME
EVEN WHEN I LEAVE HIM BEHIND
HE IS WITH ME IN THE HOME
HE HAVE NEVER LEFT ME ALONE...

WHEN I'M SICK
AND HAVING BAD FEELINGS
GOD CAME AND HEALED ME
BEFORE THE DAY HAD PASSED...

GOD IS WITH ME
WHEN I'M ASLEEP LATE AT NIGHT
THE ANGELS WATCH OVER MY BE
THE ANGELS ARE ALWAYS IN SIGHT...

written by: Ora Irving

Ora Mae Irving

"WHEN YOUR NAME IS CALLED"

WHEN YOUR NAME IS CALLED
ON THAT DAY IT WILL BE
SPECIAL TO HEAR THE WORD'S GOD SAY...

YOU NEED TO BE READY
WHEN YOUR NAME IS CALLED
GET UP IMMEDIATELY SO YOU WANT FALL...

GOD IS LOOKING AT YOU
AND HE KNOWS YOUR NAME
LIVING WITH HIM AND FOR HIM
YOU DON'T HAVE TO BE ASHAMED...

written by: Ora Irving

"ANGELS COMING FOR ME"

ANGELS ARE COMING FOR ME VERY SOON
I HAVE FINISHED MY WORK ON EARTH
WHERE THERE IS NO MORE ROOM...

I MUST GO WITH THE LORD UP THERE
I'VE FINISHED MY TEST
ANGELS ARE GOING TO TAKE ME
TO GET MY REST...

I HATE TO LEAVE YOU ALL BEHIND
I MUST GO NOW
I DON'T HAVE ANY MORE TIME...

YOU DON'T HAVE TO WORRY ABOUT ME
I'M GOING HOME WHERE NO MORE PAINS
AND I'LL NEVER BE ALONE...

written by: Ora Irving

Ora Mae Irving

"WHEN I MISSED GOD'S SPIRIT"

WHEN I MISSED GOD'S SPIRIT
COME BY MY WAY
I DON'T KNOW WHAT
TO DO OR NEVER SAY...

I SEARCH FOR AN ANSWER
TO SEE WHAT WAS WRONG
GOD'S SPIRIT STILL THERE WAITING
HAS NEVER LEFT ME ALONE...

I'LL GO BACK TO SEE
WHAT I HAVE DONE
HIS SPIRIT WAITING FOR ME
TO COME BACK HOME...

GOD WANTS ME TO BE TRUE AS CAN BE
ASKING FOR GUIDANCE TO WALK WITH ME...

written by : Ora Irving

"GOD IS WITH ME"

GOD IS WITH ME
NO MATTER WHERE I GO
HE'S WITH ME
EVEN WHEN I'M SLOW...

GOD IS WITH ME
WHEN I AM WRONG
HE EVEN STAYS WITH ME
WHEN I AM STRONG...

I CAN LOOK TO HIM
ON MY SICK DAYS
STILL CAN LOOK TO HIM
WHEN EVER I PRAY...

GOD IS WITH ME
IN MY HOME
NO MATTER WHAT ROOM I AM IN
AND HOW LONG...

GOD IS WITH ME ALL OF THE MOMENTS OF MY
LIFE
EVEN WHEN OTHERS HAS PUSHED ME ASIDE...

written by: Ora Irving

Ora Mae Irving

"MY CHILD, GO ON"

MY CHILD, GO ON DON'T STOP
KEEP ON SEARCHING
AND MAKE IT TO THE TOP...

DON'T WAIT TO LATE
UNTIL THE ROAD GET TOUGH
OR WHEN EVER
YOUR TRIALS GET ROUGH...

KEEP ON CLIMBING
TO A HIGHER HEIGHT
THEN ONE DAY
YOU WILL SEE THE BRIGHT LIGHT...

KEEP STILL AND GIVE YOUR BEST
GOD IS THERE
AND HE WILL DO THE REST...

written by: Ora Irving

"MY SECRET ROOM"

MY SECRET ROOM IS JUST FOR ME
SO I CAN THINK, WRITE, AND BE FREE...

THERE IS A PART WHERE WORDS COME TO ME
AND BE MY GUIDE
I'M WRITING AND SITTING
TO TOUCH OTHER'S LIVES...

THE ONE I LOVE
IT'S ALL COMING FROM GOD ABOVE
LIKE SOME ANGELS LYING IN A MANSION...

I'M SEARCHING AND WAITING FOR AN ANSWER
FROM THAT SECRET, I DIDN'T MENTION...

written by: Ora Irving

Ora Mae Irving

"I'M TRYING TO CHANGE"

I HAVE TRIED TO CHANGE
ON MY OWN
WALKING AND RUNNING
AND SITTING IN THE SUN...

THINGS ARE UP IN MY LIFE
SOMETIME DOWN
WHEN I REST FOR A WHILE, I'M TIRED...

WANT TO FIND A HOME TO CALL MY OWN
NOTHING WAS PROMISED
THE DAY I WAS BORN...

TROUBLE INSIDE SOMETIME
ALL WAYS DIFFERENT HELP I WANT TO FIND...

I DON'T KNOW WHAT TO DO
ASKING GOD FOR HELP
HE NEVER HAS LEFT...

written by: Ora Irving

"BEST WISHES"

BEST WISHES
GOES OUT TO YOU
IN THIS WORLD
WITHOUT ANY CLUE...

YOU ARE GREAT
WHEN EVER I SEE YOU
NO MATTER WHAT PROBLEM
YOU'RE GOING THROUGH...

YOU'RE THE BEST
ALL YEAR ROUND
I LIKE TO SEE YOU
WHEN I COME TO TOWN...

NEVER CHANGE
OR SAY BAD WORDS
WHAT COMES BY YOUR PATH
LIKE EVEN A FLYING BIRD...

YOU'RE CHEERFUL AS CAN BE
IN YOU HOME OR SITTING UNDER THE TREE...

written by: Ora Irving

"BLACK MAGIC"

BLACK MAGIC IS MOVING ALL AROUND
BY MAGICIANS ALL OVER TOWN...

HELPING THE PEOPLE WITH DISAPPEARING
OBJECTS BRINGING THEIR MIND
TO WONDER TO ASSURE HELP IS COMING...

A FORM OF PEACE
TO RELIEVE YOUR MIND
THE SOUND OF MELODY
YOU SHOULD BE ABLE TO FIND...

SOFTLY MUSIC YOU WILL FIND
THE TIME YOU SETTLE DOWN
YOU WILL BE SO KIND...

THE SPIRIT WILL FREE
YOUR EVERY DESIRE
YOU WILL REST AND WANT TO CRY...

written by: Ora Irving

"I'VE DONE MY BEST"

I'VE DONE MY BEST
YOU ALL CAN SEE
GOD CALLED ME HOME
TO SET ME FREE...

YOU CAN PLEASE AND SERVE GOD
EVEN THOUGH I'M LEAVING YOU HERE
IN THIS WORLD AND HAVE NO FEAR...

PLEASE DON'T CRY
AND SHED MANY TEARS
I'M JUST RESTING
BUT I'M STILL NEAR...

ON THIS JOURNEY
I CAME A LONG WAY
I'M RESTING WITH MY FATHER
EACH AND EVERYDAY...

I'M IN HEAVEN
AND MY BEST HAD END AT LAST
LEAVING THE WORLD BEHIND AND THE PAST...

written by: Ora Irving

"HELP OTHERS"

GOD GAVE US A GIFT
TO HELP ONE ANOTHER
LOOKING ON PEOPLE
AS YOUR SISTER OR BROTHER...

WE CAN SHOW LOVE LIKE NEVER BEFORE
WAITING TO HEAR
A KNOCK AT THE DOOR...

HELPING OTHERS IS SPECIAL
AS CAN BE
BEING KIND TO ONE ANOTHER
WILL SET YOU FREE...

LOOK BEYOND THE FAULTS
IN ANY OF THEM
GOD KNOWS WHAT'S BEST
AS A FRIEND...

HE CAN HELP YOU LIKE NO OTHER
AND DOWN THE ROAD
HE WILL KEEP YOU OUT OF TROUBLE
AND MOVE BURDENS AND HEAVY LOADS...

written by: Ora Irving

"WHEN I HAVE PASSED"

WHEN I HAVE PASSED
AND LEFT THIS WORLD
ALWAYS REMEMBER
I PUT GOD FIRST...

HE WAS THE ANSWER
TO ALL MY NEEDS
WITHOUT GOD
I WASN'T PLEASED...

HE WENT WITH ME EVERY DAY
EVEN WHEN I WAS ON MY KNEES TO PRAY...

I LOVE ALL MY FRIENDS EVERYWHERE
I DIDN'T FORGET GOD
HE WAS ALWAYS FIRST...

written by: Ora Irving

Ora Mae Irving

"I FOUND PEACE"

**I FOUND PEACE
IN MY HEART
WHEN I LOOK TO JESUS
EVERYTHING WAS SOLVED...**

**THE PEACE I FOUND
WAS SO GREAT
I STARTED ON TIME
BEFORE IT WAS TOO LATE...**

**JESUS WAS PLEASED WITH ME
TO DO EVERYTHING HE SAID
WHEN I KEPT GOING
EVERYTHING WAS ALREADY MADE...**

**I FOUND PEACE
THE VERY NEXT DAY
WHEN I FOUND JESUS
AND DONE WHAT HE SAID...**

written by: Ora Irving

"AS I WRITE"

I WRITE THE THOUGHT THAT COMES
TO ME, THE GIFT OF POEMS
THAT ARE READ IN MY HOME...

MY MIND IS FOCUSED
ON POEMS THAT COMES MY WAY
GOD'S GIVEN ME THE STRENGTH
TO HEAR WHAT WORDS TO SAY...

I WRITE ALL THE TIME
BECAUSE ALINE OF POEMS
ALWAYS ARE ON MY MIND...

written by: Ora Irving

Ora Mae Irving

"MY CHOICE OF PEACE"

MY CHOICE OF PEACE
I CHOSE EVERYDAY
TO WALK STRAIGHT
AS I PRAY...

I WILL HAVE A PATH
THAT YOU WILL WANT TO FOLLOW
DON'T NEED ANY MONEY OR
A PAPER OR A DOLLAR...

PEACE COMING DOWN
AND WITHIN A SOUL
THAT IS PRECIOUS AND HAS NO SIN...

SMILING EVERYDAY
WHEN FRIENDS SEE YOU
THAT'S A PATTERN
THEY WILL LOVE TO DO...

written by: Ora Irving

"THE BACK STAGE"

THE BACK STAGE
WHERE THERE IS HOPE
KEEP GOING ON AND STEADY GROW...

YOU ARE MOVING EVERYDAY
TRING TO COME TO THAT PLACE
WHEN STANDING IN LINE AND BEING ON TIME...

THE TERMINATION IS ALL YOU NEED
AND BEING SUCCESSFUL
SITTING AND PLEASED...

YOU ARE WONDERING OF THE CHOICE
YOU MADE TO GO ON
THE TOP AND MANY OF PLACES...

written by: Ora Irving

"ANGEL'S LOVE PEOPLE"

THE LOVE OF PEOPLE
COMING FROM WITHIN
TO HELP THEM EVERY DAY
AND TO KNOW WHEN...

YOU DO ALL THE THINGS
WITH YOUR WINGS
WHILE THE ANGELS ARE STANDING
AND SINGING JUST LIKE A KING...

THEY ARE WATCHING OVER YOU
FROM DAY TO NIGHT
WITH THE HELP FROM GOD
AND A BRIGHT STAR...

WRAPPING THEIR WINGS
NEVER GET OUT YOUR SIGHT
TRYING TO SHOW YOU LOVE
AND A VERY BRIGHT LIGHT...

written by: Ora Irving

"THE SPIRIT FROM GOD"

THE SPIRIT FROM GOD
IS WITH YOU ALWAYS
JUST PRAY AND HEAR
WHAT HE HAS TO SAY...

HE DIRECTS YOUR PATH
WHEN GOING OUT
GOD IS THERE
NEVER OUT OF YOUR SIGHT...

HE IS WAITING ON A CHANCE
TO BE IN YOUR LIFE
GIVING YOU FAITH AND
BEING A GUIDE...

GOD DOESN'T CHANGE
NO MATTER WHAT YOU DO
JUST HAVE A PLACE IN YOUR HEART
SO HE CAN SEE YOU THROUGH...

written by: Ora Irving

"THE WOMAN WITH A BIG HEART"

THE WOMAN WITH A BIG HEART
ALL THE TIME, TURNING NO ONE AWAY
KEEPING EVERYONE AROUND...

TRYING TO ENCOURAGE THEIR FAITH
BY LISTENING AND HEARING
EVERY WORD THEY SAY...

TELLING THEIR LOVE ONES
TO KEEP MOVING ON
AFTER FAME AND MONEY
IT WILL BE ON TIME AND COME...

GATHER EVERYTHING THAT
COMES BY HERE PATH
WHERE THERE IS HOPE IT WILL LAST...

NEVER GIVE UP
NO MATTER HOW THINGS ARE
THE PEACE WITHIN
WILL NEVER BE FAR...

written by: Ora Irving

"HELP IS HERE TODAY"

HELP IS HERE TODAY
CAN'T YOU SEE
PLACES TO GO
SO YOU CAN BE FREE...

HELP COMES FROM FAMILIES
AND FRIENDS
THERE BY YOUR SIDE
TO THE END...

HELP WILL LAST
AS YOU ASK
DON'T HAVE NO PRICE
IT'S NOT A TASK...

HELP WILL SPREAD
COMING FROM DEEP WITHIN
YOU CAN SEE AND KNOW
WHERE AND WHEN...

written by: Ora Irving

Ora Mae Irving

"PEOPLE OF THIS WORLD"

PEOPLE OF THIS WORLD IS SPECIAL
WITH A SWEETHEART AND GOD IS THERE
AND EVERYWHERE...

HE LOVE THEM LIKE YOU TOO
GOD NEVER CHANGE
NO MATTER WHAT YOU ARE GOING THROUGH...

PEOPLE ARE DIFFERENT
ALL OVER THIS WORLD
GOD IS IN CHARGE EVEN
IF YOU ARE TORN APART...

PEOPLE ARE WONDERFUL
ALL OVER THIS CITY
YOU HAVE TO FIND THEM
AND NOT BE BITTER...

written by: Ora Irving

"GOD HAS GIVE ME A SPEECH"

GOD HAVE GIVEN ME A SPEECH
THAT I CAN SHARE
IT WILL HELP YOUR LIFE
AND BURDENS THAT YOU BARE...

THE SPEECH IS SIMPLE
AND VERY PLAIN
GOD WANT ME TO TELL YOU
HE WILL ALWAYS REMAIN THE SAME...

HE WILL NEVER STOP LOVING YOU
BECAUSE YOU FAIL TO BE TRUE
HE WILL PROVIDE AND SEE YOU THROUGH...

HE WILL SPEAK TO ME
NO MATTER WHERE I GO
WANT ME TO BE EXAMPLES
AND NOT TO PUT ON ANY SHOW...

written by: Ora Irving

Ora Mae Irving

"HATE YOU DON'T NEED"

HATE YOU DON'T NEED
IN YOUR EVERYDAY LIFE
ASK THE LORD
TO TAKE IT AWAY WHEN IT ARRIVES...

HATE TRIES TO TAKE
OVER YOUR LIFE
FALL ON YOUR KNEES
AND HAVE THE LORD ON YOUR SIDE...

HATE YOU DON'T NEED
EVEN THOUGH YOU PRAY
HATE WILL MAKE YOU GO ASTRAY...

HATE WILL LEAVE YOU
ALL ALONG
WITH THE DEVIL LAUGHING
WHEN THINGS GO WRONG...

HATE YOU DON'T NEED
WHILE YOU'RE SITTING IN CHURCH
THE DEVIL'S POINTING HIS FINGERS
TRYING TO GET YOU, WHERE IT HURTS...

written by: Ora Irving

"A NEW HOME ABOVE"

THERE IS A NEW HOME ABOVE...
FAR BEYOND THIS WORLD...
YOU CAN SEE ONE DAY...
IF YOU LIVE BY GOD'S WORD...

THERE ARE SO MANY THINGS...
YOU HAVE NEVER SEEN BEFORE...
IF YOU WALK WITH JESUS...
THERE WILL BE NO MORE HEAVY LOADS...

SOME OF YOUR LOVES ONES...
MAY BE THERE IN THAT PLACE...
WHERE YOU WILL GO AND NEVER AGE...

FLOWERS YOU WILL SEE EVERYWHERE...
WALKING DOWN THAT PATH...
IT WILL BE THE BEST EXPERIENCE...
THAT YOU HAVE EVER HAD...

written by: Ora Irving

Ora Mae Irving

ABOUT THE AUTHOR

ORA M. IRVING
Tampa, FL

I, Ora Irving, live in Tampa, FL. I was born in Gainesville, FL. I finished high school and went to college for business management. I am currently a housewife, which I spend my time writing lyrics for songs and poems. I have received a diploma from the Poetry Society of America. I believe poetry is a gift from God, and I am thankful God chose me to write through to his people. I wrote these poems, because God has always been the head of my life. As a child my mother taught me that God was the way of life and through him all things are possible. I would like to thank God for my mother, because she motivated me to be the best I can be, and to never forget God who's the head of my life. I would also like to thank God for my sister Miriam who prayed for me everyday and who wanted what was best for me. I believe God blessed me with the talent to write poetry and through him, I will continue to write, and perhaps my poetry will inspire or touch another person's life.